Standing On One Foot

Kenneth Jernigan
Editor

Large Type Edition

A KERNEL BOOK
published by
NATIONAL FEDERATION OF THE BLIND

Table of Contents

Kenneth Jernigan, President Emeritus
National Federation of the Blind

EDITOR'S INTRODUCTION

When we started publishing the Kernel Books in 1991, we thought the series might run to three or four volumes and a modest circulation. Now, over three years later, we are issuing the sixth Kernel Book, and our circulation is approaching two and a half million. This represents a substantial amount of both work and resources, but we think the effort has been eminently worthwhile.

I have been asked why we chose the name Kernel Books, and there are a number of answers. In the first place, I suppose it has to do with whim. I thought the title was catchy, so I used it. But there is something more. We wanted to go to the very heart of blindness, trying to show our readers what it's really like—and, for that matter, what it isn't like.

If you are blind, what do you think and how do you look at things (not how do you look at them physically, but your point of view and perspective)? How about dating and marriage? What about children, recreation, work, and relations with others? In short, how do blind people live and feel on a daily basis? What we are trying to do is to cut through the sentimentality and misconceptions to the very "kernel" of the subject.

I do a lot of traveling throughout the country, and until recently, people in airports and on the streets who struck up conversations recognized me (assuming that they recognized me at all) because they had heard me on radio or seen me on television talking about the National Federation of the Blind.

Now, that has largely changed. More often than not, I meet people who have read one or another of the Kernel Books. They tell me that they feel personally acquainted with those whose stories have been told. They also feel comfortable talking about blindness—asking about the little things, such as how clothes are selected and matched, or how a blind person does grocery shopping.

This is exactly what we hoped would happen, and I think the present Kernel Book will be no exception. In its pages you will meet a blind father and a sighted mother who, with some difficulty, adopted a baby. You will experience with a blind college student his attempts to come to terms with himself and his blindness, and you will go to the courtroom with a blind woman as she is called to serve on a jury. Of course, you will also get further acquainted with people you have met in previous volumes.

As to the title of this book (*Standing on One Foot*), it comes from one of my own experiences. All of us are products of the culture in which we live, and that is true of me as well as anybody else. Therefore, although I have spent most of my life trying to help people understand the facts about blindness, I found myself sometime ago falling into the same trap that I have been urging others to avoid. It caused a good deal of soul-searching—but enough! You'll find the details in the following pages.

As I have already said, we want you to know about blindness, but we also want you to know about the National Federation of the Blind. Established in 1940, the Federation has, in the opinion of most of us who know about such things, been the single most important factor in helping blind people live normal lives and do for themselves. We who are blind still have a long way to go, but we are getting there—and the Kernel Books are helping. The reason they are helping is that they are one of the major factors in our campaign to increase public understanding and awareness. We are truly changing what it means to be blind, and you who read these books are helping. May you enjoy this book, and may you find it worthwhile.

Kenneth Jernigan
Baltimore, Maryland
1994

WHY LARGE TYPE

The type size used in this book is 14 Point for two important reasons: One, because typesetting of 14 Point or larger complies with federal standards for the printing of materials for visually impaired readers, and we wanted to show you exactly what type size is necessary for people with limited sight.

The second reason is because many of our friends and supporters have asked us to print our paperback books in 14 Point type so they too can easily read them. Many people with limited sight do not use Braille. We hope that by printing this book in a larger type than customary, many more people will be able to benefit from it.

Kenneth Jernigan stands on his hands at age 18 on his parents' farm near Beech Grove, Tennessee.

STANDING ON ONE FOOT

by Kenneth Jernigan

We who are blind are part of the larger society. We tend to see ourselves as others see us. We tend to accept the false views about our limitations and, thus, do much to make those limitations a reality.

I can offer a personal example. Quite sometime back, an article written by R. H. Gardner appeared in the *Baltimore Sun*. It was headlined: "Ice Castles' A Little Hard to Swallow," and this is what it said:

Several years ago, I was at a party when a friend, for reasons I cannot recall, bet me I could not stand on one foot 15 seconds with my eyes closed. I had been quite an athlete in my youth (10 years old), during which period I could stand on practically any part of my anatomy—head, hands, ears, or toes—for an indefinite length of time.

I accepted the bet.

To my astonishment, at the count of five I began to waver. At seven, the waver turned into a stagger; and at ten I was lost. It was a great shock for a former athlete (even a 10-year-old one), and I have never forgotten it.

For something happens to your balance when you close your eyes. And how much worse it must be if you're blind!

Being blind, a scientist-friend once pointed out to me, cannot be compared to closing your eyes. When you close your eyes, you still see. You see the undersides of the lids with the light behind them.

But what you see when you're blind is what you see out of the back of your head. There's neither light nor sight of any kind.

I was reminded of all this while watching 'Ice Castles,' a film about a blind figure skater.... I'm told there is a blind figure skater upon whose career the film is loosely based. But it's hard to believe, in view of my experience trying to stand on one leg...

When I read that article, I pooh-poohed it and laughed it to scorn. So did one of my sighted associates. Then, just to show how silly it was, she closed her eyes and stood on one foot. But the laughter stopped, for she wobbled and fell. Then, she opened her eyes and tried it again. There was no problem. She kept her balance without difficulty.

"Nonsense!" I said. "Let me show you"—whereupon, I stood on one foot—and immediately lost my balance. That incident occurred many years ago, but I still remember it as if it had happened yesterday. Was I shaken? You bet!

After getting over the shock, I did some serious soul-searching. We know that the tests which are made by blindfolding sighted people to determine what the blind can do are totally invalid. I have been among the most vocal in pointing that out. I knew (or, at least, I thought I knew) that balance is a matter of the inner ear, not the eye. Why, then, did my associate fall when her eyes were closed but keep her balance when they were open? Perhaps the fact that she was accustomed to seeing things around her as part of her daily life made the difference, or perhaps (even though she is well versed in our philosophy) the matter went deeper. Perhaps (reacting to social conditioning) she subconsciously expected to fall and was tense. I suggested that she practice a few times with her eyes closed. And what do you know? It worked. In four or five times she could stand on one foot as easily with her eyes closed as open.

But what about me? I have never had any problem with balance. In fact, I was formerly able to walk across an entire room on my hands. So I tried standing on one foot again—and I could do it with perfect ease. If anybody doubts it, I will be glad to demonstrate. Then why did I fall the first time? I reluctantly conclude that (despite all of my philosophy and knowledge to the contrary, despite all of my experience with this very sort of situation dressed out in other forms) I fell into the trap of social conditioning. I hope I won't do it again, but I can't be sure. There is probably not a blind person alive in the world today who has not, at one time or another, sold himself or herself short and accepted the public misconceptions about how limited blind people are, usually without ever knowing it. Prejudice is subtle, and tradition runs deep.

Which brings me back to Mr. Gardner and his newspaper article. He was not trying to hurt the blind, but just to make a living. Nevertheless, based on his single false experience as a simulated blind person, he made sweeping generalizations about our lacks and losses. Do you think he would believe we are capable of equality—that we can travel alone, compete with others for a regular job, and live full and normal lives? Of course not. And his opinions count. He is a member of the press, a molder of thought. And how do you think he would react if one of us brought all of this to his attention?

Probably with defensiveness and resentment. Perhaps he would even help stimulate unfavorable publicity about us, not realizing or admitting why he was doing it—or, for that matter, that he *was* doing it. Of course, he might not behave that way at all. He might learn from the experience and be a better person for it.

A few years ago I went to a cafeteria with a sighted friend. We took our trays and moved down the line. When we turned from the cash register and started for the table, an accident occurred. A glass of water fell from the tray and splashed on the floor. "There will be those," I said, "who will see this and think the reason I spilled that glass of water is because I am blind."

"You are right," my sighted friend replied; "for you didn't spill it. I did. It fell from my tray, not yours."

All of this was bad enough, but there was more, and worse. I didn't leave it there: "How did you do that?" I asked.

This time my friend (who is as well versed in our notions about blindness as I am) responded with more than a touch of acid: "I did it the same way anybody else would," she said. "I tipped my tray. Do you think it is normal for the blind to be clumsy and the sighted to be graceful? Do you think sighted people don't have accidents? Why did you automatically assume that you were the one who spilled the water?

It was a fair question, and it caused a lot of reflection. I reluctantly concluded that (despite all of my philosophy and knowledge to the contrary, despite all of my experience with this very sort of situation dressed out in other forms) I fell into the trap of social conditioning. I hope I won't do it again, but I can't be sure. The force of cultural conditioning is powerful, and changes in public attitudes about blindness are hard to set in motion.

If I, who have spent most of my life dealing with the problems of blindness, make such mistakes, how can I blame sighted people when they misjudge or fail to understand? Even though there are still a lot of wrong notions about blindness and what blind people can't do, we are learning and truly making progress. Whether sighted or blind, we should take pride in our accomplishments, but we should mix that pride with a little humility. We should have faith in ourselves and keep both feet firmly on the ground, but we should also know that sometimes we will be found standing on one foot.

NIGHTS OF WALKING

by Marc Maurer

As readers of the Kernel Books know, Marc Maurer is President of the National Federation of the Blind. He is also the father of two active, lovable children. His recollections of the birth of his son emphasize again the innate normality of the blind—the concern with the everyday activities of employment, marriage, home life, and children—the lack of the feeling that blindness is the center of every activity and the cause of doom.

Since I am a lawyer, I do a lot of traveling. I was away in Idaho working on a case when our first child, David, was born. My wife Patricia and I live in Maryland, more than 2,000 miles from Idaho. I had a hearing on Monday morning, and I needed to interview witnesses and prepare argument for the case. My wife had been pregnant for several months, but the baby wasn't supposed to arrive for quite a while. When I left on Friday morning, everything was fine. When I spoke with Patricia on Friday night, she was feeling better than she had for weeks. I went to bed more than 2,000 miles from home ready to buckle down to do the work for the court appearance scheduled for Monday.

Early Saturday morning I commenced interviews with witnesses. The trial would focus on the constitutional rights of private citizens to free speech and freedom of assembly. I was preparing testimony for the court and marshalling arguments for the summation. The court appearance would be brief—not more than half a day. A number of the facts to be presented were quite unusual, and the time before the judge would be severely limited. Preparation and planning were absolutely vital.

A number of the witnesses and I were in the living room of the home of one of the parties when I was summoned to the phone. The voice of one of my best friends (Dr. Kenneth Jernigan, who was then serving as president of the National Federation of the Blind) came on the line. He said, "Don't worry. You are a papa. Everybody's fine!"

Immediately, the focus of my attention shifted. The court hearing had to be completed, and the planning and preparation were no less important, but I felt a tremendous urge to head back to Baltimore. All through Saturday and Sunday as I worked on the case, I thought about my new baby boy and his mom. The hearing occurred on schedule Monday morning, and as soon as it was over, I boarded a plane headed east.

It is a long way from Boise to Baltimore. The plane touched down about 11:30 that night, and a friend picked me up and drove me to the hospital. My wife was tired but glad to see me. She told me that there were those at the hospital who had been wondering whether I really existed. Baby Maurer had not yet been named. We decided to call him David Patrick.

Because our new boy was premature (he weighed less than four pounds), he had been assigned to live in a little plastic box called an isolette, which had wires and dials. The isolette had its own heating and air conditioning system, which was set to keep the boy warmer than ordinary room temperature. Some time around 12:30 a.m. I went in to visit him. I was instructed by the hospital staff to wear a gown and to make sure my hands were clean. David Patrick was little and scrawny. He wore a teeny little cap to keep him warm, along with his blankets and diaper. I sat there with him in a rocking chair for some time, but he didn't have very much to say. I asked him where he wanted to go to college, but I guess he hadn't made up his mind. Because he was so small (his leg bones from his knees to his ankles felt sort of like match sticks to me). The hospital had tiny little preemie diapers for him. They looked like toys you might get for the baby doll that you give as a Christmas present. David Patrick got himself all wet, and the nurse asked me if I wanted to change him. The door to the isolette opened out to make a little shelf. The idea was that David

Patrick's blankets should be spread on the shelf and he should be placed upon them to be changed. I put him on the shelf and took off his diaper. Then I crouched down to get at the cabinet underneath to get him a new one. The nurse said to me, "Watch it! He might roll off!" The nurse's voice was not loud, but it carried considerable force. Accidents can happen, and a fall of three feet for a baby of that size could cause severe damage. Those few words from the nurse were stern and to the point. My job was to keep track of that boy. So I reached up over the shelf and took hold of the little guy.

With the diaper changed, the blankets back in place, and the hat back on (it had fallen off during the changing process), we sat peacefully a while longer. I told David Patrick about the cases I was involved in. We discussed politics, crops, the economic situation in the country, and the weather. At about 2 o'clock I told him I'd have to go because there was another busy day ahead. But I told him I'd be back, and he seemed to know that I would.

At the time David Patrick was born, I was building a law practice. Each day I would go to the office, deal with clients, draft motions and petitions, make court appearances, accomplish necessary travel either within the state of Maryland or throughout the country, deal with other lawyers, and conduct my everyday business. Each night (when I wasn't on the road) I would visit the hospital to see how David Patrick was doing—he stayed for a month after he was born. Patricia and I were working full time each day—she as an administrator of programs for the blind, and I as a lawyer. David Patrick stayed with the baby sitter during the day. When we brought him home in the evening, he was often hungry and sometimes sleepy. During the night he slept just like a baby—that is, he woke up and cried every two hours. Sometimes he wanted to eat; sometimes he needed clean clothes; often he needed both food and clothes. Many nights he just wanted company. Occasionally, he would let me rock him in the rocking chair—where I could

*Marc, Patricia, and
David Patrick Maurer.*

doze. However, there were times that he wanted to be walked. I never could find a way to sleep while walking the baby—up and down, up and down. I did learn to sleep almost everywhere else. My colleagues came to know that if we were riding in an elevator in a 20 story building, I would sometimes take a brief nap on the way up.

The doctors were afraid that David might be subject to Sudden Infant Death Syndrome. This is a condition which causes the heart and lungs to stop functioning long enough that the baby dies. Consequently, David Patrick was required to wear a heart and respiratory monitor. The heart monitor had two major parts. There was a belt that wrapped around the baby's chest. On the belt were three small electrodes. Wires attached to these electrodes plugged into a box that had switches and displays on it. If David's pulse stopped or his breathing was interrupted, the monitor would beep. Patricia and I took a course to tell us what to do in case of an emergency. The first step was to take David Patrick and give him a good shake. The heart monitor would also sound if one of the electric leads to the monitoring belt came loose.

During the first month that our son was home, the device sounded several times, but these were all false alarms. It wasn't always a false alarm, however. One night the monitor woke us from a deep sleep. I jumped up and found that David Patrick was not breathing. I wondered if I could remember all the steps we had learned in the course to revive an infant. The first step was to shake the baby. I was ever so grateful that step number one worked. David Patrick received a thorough shaking. He complained about it, but he had to breathe to do it.

David Patrick was the first child, and Dianna Marie came three years later. Today they are both in school and doing fine. You would never know that both of them were premature. The children and I still talk about crops and politics and the weather, but there are other topics of conversation—homework, Boy and Girl Scout activities, trumpet lessons, making fudge, and visits to Grandma. Even though both Patricia and I are blind, our children are not. Sometimes the subject of blindness is part of the conversation.

When I was six, I was enrolled at a boarding school for the blind, which was many miles from our home. My parents took me there and left me to stay in the dormitory. I was homesick, but my father had told me that he would be back to bring me home the next weekend. When Friday came, he was there. During the next four years my father came every other Friday to pick me up and take me home. I knew I could count on him. I looked forward to his coming, and I planned for the long trip home. He might not be able to be with me as much as he would have liked, but he'd be there on Fridays.

Both of my parents were like that. Once my mother told me that no doctor could work on me unless we had talked about it and she had given her permission. At the school for the blind I got tonsillitis and was sent to the hospital. Officials at the school told me that an operation would be necessary. I knew that my mother had promised me that no one could work on me unless we'd talked about it and she had given her consent. I was told by the hospital officials on a Tuesday night that the operation would occur the next morning. Early on Wednesday my mother came to my bedside. She and my father had driven much of the night in order to come to the hospital. They told me that the operation was really necessary and that I would be all right. I felt much relieved—especially because my mother had done what she had told me she would.

The quality of being reliable is fundamental. I have tried to emulate my father and mother in this respect. When I have promised my children that a thing will happen, I have tried to make it come true. And when they have needed my support, I have tried to give it.

There is an oft-repeated saying, which is that nothing comes free. The folksy expression is, "There ain't no such thing as a free lunch." Each individual must pay for what he or she gets.

However, children demand much from their parents and others. They need to be nurtured, fed, clothed, walked through the wee hours of the night, bathed, entertained, directed, and taught. They take inordinate amounts of time, energy, concentration, and money. And, they have nothing tangible with which to pay. However, there is one commodity which they possess in abundance—love. Despite all the troubles and trials, the children give at least as good as they get. They provide something which can be had in no other way. They add an irreplaceable element to the warmth and the caring of the home.

I take family life for granted today, but it wasn't always that way. Before I came to be a part of the National Federation of the Blind, I wondered very often whether there would be a future for me. Today, I know that there is, and I work within the organization to help other blind people come to the same realization. We in the National Federation of the Blind are in many ways a family of our own. We have warmth and caring for each other, and we work to bring opportunities to blind people who have been afraid they might not have a future. One of the characteristics which is most notable about our organization is that if a blind person is willing to work and needs our help, we do what we can to give it. The National Federation of the Blind is always willing to be supportive to blind people who are working hard to gain independence and a positive future.

Dr. Homer Page

YOU'RE GOING FOR ALL OF US

by Homer Page

Homer Page is totally blind. He is a university professor and an elected official in his community. He attributes much of his success in life to his mother, who also happens to be blind. Here he tells his mother's story.

D'Arline Creech was born on September 12, 1915. She came into this world in a small farm house near Troy, Missouri. She attended school in a one room schoolhouse, no more than three hundred feet from the place she was born. In many ways her life was uneventful, but in many other ways she represents some of the strongest dimensions of the human experience. It is her story that I want to tell. It is a special story to me because D'Arline Creech Page is my mother.

Blindness is a condition that has existed in my family for many generations. There are at least six generations of us who have learned to live positive, productive lives as blind persons. I am the first in this line who has received an education and made my way in the broader world. Much of this is due to the changing times and to the effect that the National Federation of the Blind has had on the attitudes of our society. Yet one does not make a successful life without being grounded in a strong personal identity drawn from past generations.

I am 50 years old. I have been blind from birth. I have earned a Ph.D., and I have lettered in wrestling at a major university. I have taught in universities and I currently serve as a County Commissioner in Boulder County, Colorado. My life has been enriched by friends and family from across this nation and the world. I now have a grandson who at this writing is six months of age. As I look back on my life and my blindness, I become more and more aware of the way in which my mother taught me to have pride and worth as a blind person.

My mother was born on the same farm in Missouri where I was born. She always had very low vision, but as she grew older, her vision decreased. She dropped out of school after the tenth grade and lived a very limited life for the next ten years. Her mother was also blind. They lived together after her father's death on the family farm.

During this time, my grandmother and my mother provided a home for a number of foster children. This was during the depression of the 1930's and money was very scarce. They scraped by and managed to pay the taxes on the farm and not to lose it. Many of their neighbors were not so successful.

My father and mother had grown up together and attended the same one room country school. They were married in 1940. My father had grown up as an orphan. He had made his way as a rodeo cowboy and a musician. When my mother and father were married he moved in to the family farm and took on the responsibilities of managing it.

My mother and father raised three children and improved their economic position through hard work and the careful use of the scarce resources that they had available to them. They were married over thirty-five years before they took a vacation. My mother canned fruits and vegetables each year. They grew their own meat and dairy products. We were always well fed, clean, and well loved. We never knew that we were economically deprived. We always thought that we were just fine and I think we were.

However our family had one very difficult winter. In 1947, the crops failed. My father had just returned from the army and our resources were practically non-existent. He and she went to town to find jobs. My father was hired to work on the railroad, and my mother found employment in a local garment factory. This was hard work for her. She had to cut and sew women's lingerie. She had to follow a pattern. It was stressful work. It was hard for her to keep up with the production quotas. She got paid by the piece. However, she worked all winter and with the income that they each earned, they bought cattle and seeds for the next year's crops. It was the only time that she had to work outside the home. She never complained and was glad to make her contribution. However, she was also very glad to be able to quit.

My mother was never a leader at the neighborhood church or in the local school. She was always quiet in meetings. She was not a leader in the family. She never tried to prove herself to anyone. Yet, I learned more about living productively from her than anyone else. What was it then that this simple woman offered to me that I found so valuable?

My mother looked for ways to be productive around the farm. She didn't have to look very far. She was patient. She defined the jobs that needed to be done and that she could do. She did those jobs well, and with consistent discipline for many years. She washed our clothes on a wash board. She cooked and cleaned and canned. When my father got a job as the local town marshal, she washed and ironed his uniforms with great pride. He looked very professional in his well pressed uniform, and she took great pride in that.

My mother cared for her children. She defended them as well as disciplined them. She made sure that they went to school and did their homework. She also made sure that they did their chores.

Often blind and sighted persons alike will say, "Well, what can I do, what can I do that is worthwhile and meaningful?" All too often, we fail to recognize the obvious. There are many valuable things which each of us can do if we choose to do them.

Is my mother a model for this generation of blind persons and especially for blind women? In some ways she is not. She never had an opportunity to learn Braille or to travel independently. She never went to school and developed an occupation outside the home. She was not a leader, nor was she outspoken on the issues of the time. In many ways she was dependent on others. First on her mother and then on my father. Yet in spite of all of these things that she was not, I believe that there is much that is instructive about her life.

Throughout the generations blind persons have not had the opportunity for an education or for full participation in our society. It was easy enough to sit down and allow others to care for them. Many did, but many like my mother patiently waited for the chance to serve. They found that chance in different ways. Some were street musicians—they created the blues. Others worked in sheltered workshops. Still others like my mother raised families. They were proud persons. They had belief in themselves because they knew that they were contributing. They had a kind of mental toughness that allowed them to endure through all of the self-denying experiences which was their lot in life. Even though they were dependent, and even though others may have felt sorry for them, they patiently waited and when their time came to give, they took advantage of it.

To these enumerable blind persons who (in spite of everything) found ways to be productive, those of us who have found our way in a broader world owe great debts of gratitude. They never quit trying. They were patient and they waited. When their time came they produced. Those of my generation and the generations to come have doors opened for us that those before us did not. Yet we too have our barriers to overcome—frustrations, and those stubborn, pervasive societal attitudes that would keep us dependent. From those who have gone before us we can learn endurance and patience. We can also learn the joy that one can derive from giving, from being of worth to others, and from being productive.

My mother was a very happy person. She drew joy from her family and from her sense of personal worth. She knew we needed her and that gave her great pleasure. She knew she counted. She never became cynical or depressed because she was not something other than herself. She knew she belonged. This joy and wholeness is still anther gift that the generations who have come before us can sometimes offer to us. They suffered. Their dreams were diminished because of the lack of opportunity, but they endured. My generation and those yet to come will have more opportunity. I hope they have as much joy and as much of a sense of self worth.

Often I am asked to discuss what it is like to be blind. There's always a need to try to change the attitudes of sighted and blind persons alike, so I talk about how easy it is to live as a blind person. I talk of the rather simple adaptations that allow me to do all of the things that my job and life demand. I talk of all of my blind friends who are involved in exciting, challenging careers. All of these things are true, and they will be true even in greater degrees for the generations to come because we truly are

changing what it means to be blind. Yet I
will always remember what happened when
I left home to go to college. My mother gave
me money that she had saved and said to
me, "Do well. You're going for all of us."

MY EXPERIENCE AS A JUROR

by Gwen Nelson

Gwen Nelson is a leader in the National Federation of the Blind of Virginia, and she takes her Federationism seriously. Therefore, when she received a summons to appear for jury duty, it caused her to do some soul searching. As blind people we want our rights, but we try to remember that with them comes responsibility. Here is how Gwen describes it.

One afternoon I was looking through what seemed to be a routine batch of mail when I found a rather official-looking envelope. The envelope contained a summons for me to appear for jury duty. I knew one blind person who had received this same type of summons, and that individual wrote "blind" across the envelope and returned it to the court. The individual was not contacted again.

For a brief moment I considered making the same response as my blind acquaintance. After all, I reasoned, jury duty certainly would be an inconvenience. My term was to last for a month, and I was to call a number at the court each day to hear if I was to appear. My next thought was that even if I were to appear, I would not be permitted to serve because someone might object to my serving because I am blind.

Then, as a Federationist, I was really ashamed, because many blind people before me who believe as I do that blind people should be first-class citizens, had stood by their convictions so that now I had the opportunity to accept the responsibility and privilege of taking my turn on jury duty.

Yes, I did have to wait around the court-house for hours. It was inconvenient, but I did serve on a jury. I had the assistance I needed to read printed materials submitted as evidence at the trial. And, as I look back, I am truly glad that I chose to fulfill my duty as a citizen. Jury duty was educational and rewarding. Now, when people ask me, I will have one more reason to say that I am proud to be a member of the National Federation of the Blind.

Olegario Cantos receives congratulations from President Maurer and President Emeritus Jernigan at NFB scholarship ceremony.

NO MORE HIDING

by Olegario Cantos

One of the best things about the scholarship program of the National Federation of the Blind is that in recent years we have been able to bring the young people who win scholarships to our National Convention.

Often it's the first time they have ever met successful blind adults, and the week-long experience can reverse a lifetime of fear. Olegario Cantos won a scholarship and attended the National Convention, and, as is so often the case, it changed his life. Here is how he tells it:

I was born two months prematurely. As a result I had no vision in my left eye and partial vision in my right. Since I did have a tiny bit of vision, all emphasis in my life in everything I did was placed on the use of that vision, and my attitudes were shaped accordingly.

I remember as a child what I thought about blindness. At first I did not know what blindness was. Then, as I grew older, I played with other children, children who happened to be fully sighted. They were allowed to run around, play tag, and use playground equipment. Though this was sometimes true in my case, there was a subtle difference. More often than with other children, I was either prevented from or discouraged from engaging in any vigorous activities.

"Why can't I do things like everyone else?" I asked.

The reply was, "Well you can't see too well, and there are just some things that you can't do." This was in reference to vigorous activity. Gradually I acquired a belief that I was inferior to the sighted, that having sight meant having ability, and that my lack of sight had to mean that I was not quite as capable as those with full visual capacity.

By the same token, I also felt lucky. After all, I did have some vision, unlike totally blind people. Based upon this misconception about blindness, I often remarked, "Don't accuse me of being blind; I am not helpless." This was what I believed about blindness, and it affected every area of my life. It affected what I believed about certain issues, including Braille.

When I was in first grade, I was taught how to read and write print just as were children who were sighted. At first it was slow. We were all slow because reading and writing were still new to us, but soon a gap developed. This gap between their reading and writing speed and mine began to increase.

In time fellow students became faster and faster in both reading and writing while I generally remained at the same level. In fourth grade something else happened. The print in the text books became smaller. In addition, the reading assignments were longer and more complex, requiring more time. Moreover, they were made more often than in the earlier grades.

Now I was faced with a problem. What was I to do? This material was really hard, and I had to find a way to deal with it. I thought that the most important factor was that I could read print, and I must do this at all costs so help me God, and that is what I did, for a while. I increased my use of special tools such as magnifying glasses and closed circuit televisions, and, to some degree, it did work.

However, no matter how hard I tried, I could only read very slowly—about twenty words a minute, and I could only read for about fifteen minutes at a time. Yet I was very, very happy with this performance. After all, I managed to avoid having to learn Braille, which I believed was only for totally blind people and was a last resort if a person could not read one letter of print. This conviction was strengthened by my belief that Braille was bulky and slow.

My beliefs with regard to the use of Braille also affected my belief in the use of the long white cane, or of any cane for that matter. I vowed, "I don't need to carry a cane. I will never, never carry a cane; not until the day I die will I carry a cane." Why? Because I thought people would think I was helpless, because, after all, blind people are helpless. Since I was not helpless, I felt I was not blind. Since I was not blind, I did not need to carry a cane, and I refused.

I gave little consideration to the fact that I got into more accidents than did the average sighted person, and this was not due to clumsiness. Literally, I fell down steps, tripped over curbs, and otherwise bumped into obstacles in my way that I could easily have avoided by simply walking around them.

To justify this state of affairs, I said, "Well, I don't get into accidents that often, not that often." But I did not ask myself why I should get into any accidents at all.

Then I found the National Federation of the Blind, and I attended my first national convention last year. For the first time, for the very first time, I gained a full sense of who and what I was, and I know who and what I am. I am a person who happens to be blind, equal in every way. I am equal in capability and competence. We are neither tragically deprived nor wondrously gifted. I now know, because of the National Federation of the Blind, that the obstacles that we as blind people face can be overcome.

After last year, when I returned from the NFB convention, I knew that I had a challenge ahead of me, that of telling my parents that I wasn't ashamed of being blind any longer. So when I walked in the door carrying a long white cane for the very first time, they said it was the most pitiful state in which they had ever seen me.

"You have never carried a cane in your life; why do you need one now? After all, you haven't been getting into that many accidents, and even if you were to get into some, at least you weren't carrying a cane." I asked them what was wrong with carrying a cane. They said, "If you carry a cane, don't you understand, people will think you are blind."

I said, "So people think that I am blind." They said, "But don't you see that if people think you are blind, they'll think that you are helpless." Thus raged the battle. It got to the point of a heated argument.

One of them said, "If you carry that thing when you are with me in public, I will not acknowledge that I know you." Later we had a discussion about Braille. I told my parents that I was going to learn it. They responded that Braille was just for totally blind people. "I don't want anyone to know that you are blind."

I said, "Look, all my life I have been a poor reader because I had to read print, and look where it has gotten me. I have done well enough, but I could have done better."

"Well," they said, "We are not going to budge." I said that I would not budge either. They thought they wouldn't, but they did.

They budged, and in time they grew to understand.

But I can't help thinking, if only my parents had known when I was a child, what they know now, if only they had had within them the beliefs of the National Federation of the Blind, things would have been so different in my life. They would have fought for me to learn Braille. They would have made sure that I was trained in cane travel. Most important, they would have known that it is respectable to be blind.

I AM BLIND AND A GENUINE HORSE TRADER

by Dan Crawford

Dan Crawford is the only genuine horse trader I know—blind or sighted. Since most of you probably don't know any horse traders either, I thought you might like to hear his story. Here is how he tells it:

I was born in Garden Prairie, Illinois, in a farming community and raised on a dairy farm that my parents operated. I lost my left eye at the age of five and only had ten percent vision in my right eye. I attended the Illinois Braille and Sight Saving School in Jacksonville through my sophomore year. And I guess everybody at Jacksonville could have predicted my future. I used to slip away to the local stable and eventually got caught and got in trouble. So from then on my future was definitely predictable.

At the end of my sophomore year I transferred to Belvedere High School. And it was during my junior and senior year of high school that I really started working horses.

I was very fortunate in that my father was an excellent horseman and able to teach me a lot. I also associated with qualified horse people, as well as excellent veterinarians and farriers.

I never will forget the first horse that I trained for money. I was offered $35 a month to ride this horse, and back in those days $35 was a lot of money, so I jumped at the chance. Believe me, I needed every dollar.

From then on, horses started coming in for training on a regular basis. And between training horses, helping to milk cows, and going to school I kept quite busy. After graduation I still continued to train horses. By then I'd upped my rate to $50 a month.

Then the horses still continued to come in for training. I attended college for a while

Dan Crawford

and worked horses on the side. Eventually I upped my rate to $100 a month. And people still continued to send me horses.

About this time I incorporated a new aspect of the horse business. I started buying untrained horses and training them for resale. I found that I could make far more money than I could training them for their owners. And so I continued this practice.

Then, I took a factory job working for the Green Giant Canneries, but I still worked horses on the side.

And it was about this time that some of my friends and I decided that we'd like to rodeo a little bit. We started roping and tying a little bit with Mom and Dad's dairy cows. Needless to say this did not make my mother too happy.

And about the same time one of my friends got hold of a real outstanding bareback bronco. One of the times I had my pride hurt the most was when this bronk bucked me off, kicked me in the head, and knocked me out for eight hours. Unfortunately, all of this was completely documented on color film.

Well, enough about my rodeo days. I still continued to train horses. About this time I realized that there was more money to be made in strictly buying and selling horses because there was far less chance of getting my bones broken. So I continued buying and selling horses.

But this didn't put enough bread on the table, so I took a better factory job at Belvedere Products, where I worked as an upholsterer. Fortunately the two jobs seemed to work quite well together—that is, for a few years. Eventually the horse business got big enough that I had to give up the factory job.

At this time I might add that while I was working at Belvedere Products, I lost the remaining sight in my right eye. I was twenty-seven years old, and I wondered if I'd still be able to continue the horse business. Somehow I just knew I could.

In some respects it was easier continuing the business after I lost my sight than before. During the last couple of years of seeing, I found my sight was actually more of a hindrance.

The strange thing was that all this time that I was buying, selling, and trading horses, I never thought of it as a career or anything to base a future on—just something to while away time and keep myself busy. I was probably thirty years old before it dawned on me: Well, I'm probably born to be a horse trader and probably will be the rest of my life.

And so I still continue buying and selling horses. But I also started buying and selling saddles and horse trailers. I found that the three seemed to work quite well together.

And so I practiced this for a few years and traveled around the country having a good time. But in 1975 a big change came into my life. I met my wife to be, Sue, and we were married.

At this time we specialize in the Arabian horse. I will have to admit that I am just a little bit prejudiced toward the Arabian—although, in fairness, we have owned some outstanding quarter horses, appaloosas, thoroughbreds, Tennessee Walkers, and a few Morgans, as well as a few other breeds. But our business is basically geared around the Arabian.

The next major change in our lives occurred in 1981. We moved away from Illinois and into Tennessee on a twenty-acre farm near Estill Springs. Estill is located exactly half way between Nashville and Chattanooga on Interstate 24. Our farm has four stock-filled ponds. We have in our ponds catfish, bass, and crappies, as well as a year round spring fed creek.

So I thought perhaps when we moved to Tennessee that I might retire from the horse business—strictly relax and fish and have a good time.

But as things will happen, they don't always work out that way. When I moved from Illinois, I sold every horse that we owned. But a good deal came along with some horses, and before I knew it, we were back in the horse business bigger than ever. We had to build a new barn to expand our facilities. And if all goes well, we hope to build a new house this year. It's about time. Sue deserves one.

I often have people tell me they think it's just amazing the way I handle and get along with horses. And they wonder if I think other blind people could do the same thing. And my answer is immediate. Yes.

If I were a young blind person and wanted to get into the horse business, there are ways in which I feel this could be accomplished. I would start buying and selling saddles and bridles and other related accessories. It would take approximately six months to a year to learn most of the horse equipment. But hopefully this would be a way the beginner could start to meet competent and qualified horse people and also a way for the beginner to start his or her education in becoming a genuine horse trader.

To become a horse trader it's a long drawn out process. It's just like going to college. It's going to take from three to five years to understand completely and learn the horses' anatomy and conformation, as well as various good and bad points about the horse, as well as studying up on pedigree.

So that is why I think I would start handling horse-related accessories. This would bring in a source of income while learning the business.

There is no reason why other blind people can't become genuine horse traders. The horse business is a multi-billion dollar business. And ninety to ninety-five per cent of the people who get into the business fail. Now I know that may seem hard to believe. Let me assure you that it is true. Therefore, there is money to be made for the remaining five percent. So I say if you are at all interested in becoming a horse trader, go for it.

Deborah Kent Stein

WHERE IS THE WASHROOM?

by Deborah Kent Stein

Deborah Kent Stein is a recognized professional author. She is also blind and a member of the National Federation of the Blind of Illinois. From time to time she writes profiles of fellow Federation members—always lively without being melodramatic and sensitive without being sentimental. Here is one such profile.

To this day, Bill Reif has vivid memories of the National Federation of the Blind student seminar he attended during his senior year in high school. "What they kept saying was that we had to take responsibility for ourselves," he explains. "People there were telling me I shouldn't just accept what the so-called experts said I should be doing—I should push to learn whatever skills I needed and figure out the techniques that would work best for me."

During the summer after he graduated from high school, Bill put the advice he heard at the NFB seminar into action. He knew he would have to hand in assignments in print when he started college in the fall. So he taught himself typing, a skill which the experts had somehow considered unnecessary for a blind student.

Even in high school, Bill knew that he wanted to become a lawyer. He attended the College of Du Page for two years and then transferred to Illinois Benedictine College in Lisle, where he had the chance to live away from home for the first time. After receiving his B.A., he entered law school at the University of Illinois in Champaign.

Law school was more challenging than anything he had tackled before. In college lectures he had relied heavily on his memory, but now he realized that he needed an effective way of taking notes in class. So he taught himself to write Braille using the slate and stylus.

After graduation from law school, Bill decided to look for a job in Champaign, where he had made many friends. For a while he did legal research, but he found full-time jobs were hard to come by. After two years he moved to Springfield, taking a job with the Illinois Department of Insurance, a state agency which regulates the insurance industry. The position lasted only ten months; then he was sending out resumes again.

Over the next two years Bill flooded the job market with applications and went on dozens of interviews. But employers were highly skeptical of hiring a blind lawyer. "Who brought you here?" they would ask him during interviews. "Is your mother waiting for you out there?" They questioned how he could handle travel on the job and what he would do about the heavy reading load. While Bill tried to focus attention on his professional skills and interests, the employers all too often couldn't find their way past blindness-related concerns. "You know, this building is awfully big and complicated, and the washrooms are up on the second floor...."

When a job finally came his way, it was through a fluke he could never have foreseen. A friend was taking a journalism class and wrote an article about Bill, which was published in the Springfield paper. The article was straightforward and unsentimental. It described how Bill had taught himself to cook, how he enjoyed roller skating, and how he was searching diligently for a job. A few days after the article appeared, the telephone rang. The caller was Illinois Attorney General Neil Hartigan.

"I was utterly amazed," Bill recalls. "He not only invited me to come in for an interview, he offered me a choice of working in practically any division I wanted within his office. I couldn't believe it was really happening!"

In April, 1983, Bill went to work in the Department of Consumer Protection within the Attorney General's office. "I selected that particular area because it's very deeply concerned with justice," he explains. "It's really a matter of seeing that people get their rights."

Federation philosophy has proved an asset as Bill resolves blindness-related problems on the job. Each time he has had a change of supervisor, he has had to prove his abilities over again. Some, for example, have reassigned cases which they feared would require more research than they thought he could handle. Others have been reluctant to give him direct courtroom experience. He has learned to be assertive, to explain his techniques for getting the job done, and to insist on gaining experience which will enhance his professional development. "If you're not careful," he warns, "the job will get structured according to what others think you can do."

Bill got married in 1985. He met his wife, Roberta, through the Lutheran church, where he is an active member. Their son Bruce is two years old.

Even when he planned to marry and raise a family, Bill encountered some people who told him he would never be able to manage such responsibilities. Again his personal philosophy, supported by his involvement in the National Federation of the Blind, strengthened his belief in himself. "You can't let anybody else tell you what you can do and can't do," he advises. "Be honest with yourself about your abilities and limitations but never be afraid to take chances."

SHANTHI'S FIRST AMERICAN YEAR

by Barbara Freeman

Mike Freeman, a blind computer analyst, and his wife Barbara (who is sighted) are long-time leaders in the Washington state affiliate of the National Federation of the Blind. When Mike and Barbara began the adoption process about four years ago, they were a little nervous. Not only did they have to deal with the usual bewildering mass of paperwork, interviews, and unexpected pitfalls associated with the adoption—especially overseas adoption—process, but they had to deal with questions and doubts about Mike's ability to care for a child. Why? For no other reason than the fact that Mike is blind. Fortunately, it is no longer rare or unusual for blind individuals successfully to adopt children. The National Federation of the Blind has been providing help and encouragement to prospective blind adoptive parents for over twenty years.

As a consequence, blind persons generally have fewer difficulties today in overcoming negative attitudes and ignorance about blindness among adoption social workers. So it was with Mike and Barbara, and eventually Shanthi joined her family in America. But a whole new set of challenges awaited Mike and Barbara. Shanthi, too, is blind, and for nearly a year she had been in a less than ideal environment. Here is Barbara's story of "Shanthi's First American Year."

My husband, Mike, and I met our new daughter, Shanthi Anne, at the Seattle-Tacoma International Airport on November 13, 1990. Shanthi, then aged eleven and a half months, flew to us from India. Our social worker had recommended this baby to us because she was outstandingly responsive and alert when she observed her on a trip to India the previous April. Shanthi is anophthalmic, this means she was born without eyes.

When Shanthi arrived at our home in November, she had changed little since she had been placed in the foundling home the previous April. She could not bear weight; she could sit up, but not get to a sitting position by herself; and she could roll, but not crawl or creep. She examined people's faces, hands, and clothing, but never reached out to find anything beyond the person holding her. Most disturbing of all, Shanthi did not know what a bottle was and could not use a cup or eat from a spoon.

Another set of parents had visited her foundling home and had observed the babies being fed. Because of a nipple-borne infection, the doctor had forbidden bottles. As a result, at every feeding one caretaker would hold the babies down and pry open their mouths while another caretaker would pour thick water-buffalo milk in from above. The babies would scream and gag the whole time. The social worker who brought Shanthi from India had been feeding her with a little medicine syringe. She would squirt formula into Shanthi's mouth while Shanthi sucked her thumb. Shanthi expected to be fed lying down, and never took her thumb out of her mouth. She got more formula on her than in her.

We drove home with our baby without any idea about how we were going to feed her. Upon the advice of our pediatrician, we decided to train Shanthi to a cup instead of back to a bottle. Our doctor also advised us to start feeding her a wide variety of foods immediately. Shanthi was underweight and had mild anemia. There was no time to introduce solid foods gradually. Shanthi's front teeth were coming in when she arrived so it was doubly important that she learn to bite and chew right away. A child who does not learn to use her teeth when they are coming in often has eating problems. A delay in learning how to eat plus the early trauma of forced feeding might very well have caused a life-long problem.

Thus began an extremely intense three weeks. My goals were twofold: first, to teach her how to eat a mixed diet and second, to give her control over her food intake as soon as possible. I bought training cups with lids that allowed the formula to flow when the cup was tipped. I wanted Shanthi to know that tipping the cup caused the milk to flow. Some training cups are so spill-proof that the milk must be sucked out.

I insisted from the first that Shanthi sit up to eat or drink. I sat her in my lap with my left arm behind her back so she could not lie down. By the third feeding, she was sitting in the highchair. When I gave her a drink, she learned she could control intake by pushing my hand away. I also got her to eat a little strained food but I had to chase her mouth as she moved her head back and forth. She also kept her thumb in her mouth most of the time and I had to catch her when it came out. I learned to keep the spoon in one place and let her come to it. Within ten days Shanthi could eat graham crackers and even a fig newton cookie. Upon the advice of an eating therapist, I stopped using baby-food the same day she learned how to eat the graham crackers.

I taught her how to pick up the cup by placing her hands on it and showing her what to do. After she learned how to pick it up, it took several more days to learn how to tip up the cup to get the formula. I placed crackers or large sticks of food in her hand and moved her hand from the tray to her mouth. Soon she could feed herself finger-food. As Shanthi practiced feeding herself, she slowly learned how to get smaller bits of food into her mouth. As soon as Shanthi discovered that she could feed herself, she refused to take anything from a spoon. She began to use a spoon again only when I showed her how to use it herself.

Shanthi attended the NFB National Convention in New Orleans in the summer where she became much more aware of how adults drink out of open cups because she sat in our laps a lot while we talked with friends. She heard the tinkling ice in water, juice, and tea and started reaching for them. I would help her taste them. When we got home, I taught her how to drink from an open cup. I moved her hands from behind.

Because she was having trouble moving the full cup to her mouth, I fed her a few times in just her diaper without a bib so she could feel right away what movement made the milk spill. She learned in four days.

We also began helping Shanthi with her motor skills shortly after she arrived. Shanthi began walking with us holding on with two hands in January, 1991, and could walk holding on with one hand by May. In early Fall, I taught her how to climb stairs while I held her hands.

As Shanthi's second birthday approached, she was rapidly developing new language, charm, and musical ability. Shanthi has quite a wide vocabulary now. She will ask her daddy to play the piano and says, "See book" when she comes across anything with Braille on it. She celebrated entering the "Terrible Twos" by singing the entire Star-Spangled Banner substituting "no" for each word.

Shanthi has great dignity. Her daddy and I hope to be able to teach her the skills she needs to put her proud independence into practice without crushing her spirit in the process.

I have learned that if I am to teach Shanthi a new skill, we must both be ready. I will not always know just how I, as the mother, get ready to move with Shanthi to the next phase of development. I believe my membership in the National Federation of the Blind will continue to give me the faith to believe that if I teach, she will learn.

TO SEA WITH A BLIND SCIENTIST

by Geerat J. Vermeij

Scientific research is not a career most people believe to be suitable for the blind, but such beliefs are changing. Dr. Geerat Vermeij is a nationally recognized marine biologist. He conducts research and teaches students at the doctoral level. Dr. Vermeij tells us that science is competitive, tedious, and hard—and, that he loves it. Here is what he has to say:

How, a skeptic might ask, could a blind person ever hope to be a scientist? After all, science is difficult if not impenetrable even for many sighted people; and, in any case, there is almost nothing in the way of books about science available to the blind.

How would one carry out experiments? How would one gain access to the huge scientific literature? Perhaps a blind person could be a physicist, at least a theoretical physicist, but surely not a biologist. Why would the blind willingly choose biology, that most visual of all the sciences?

The answer is very simple. Science, and for me biology in particular, is absolutely fascinating. Someone is actually paying me to study shells—some of the most beautiful works of architecture in all of nature—in the expectation that broad principles with implications for our own species will emerge.

What is more, I get to travel to exotic places, to read the scientific literature in all its fantastic diversity, to see my own papers and books published, and to teach others about science, that most powerful of all ways of knowing. What more could one ask of a profession?

Like many of my colleagues, I came to science early in life. Even as a small boy growing up in the Netherlands, I picked up shells, pine cones, pretty stones, and the like. My parents, both of whom are avid natural historians, took pains to acquaint me with all kinds of creatures that lived in the

Geerat Vermeij
examines a seashell.

grassy polders and in the innumerable ditches that crisscrossed the Low Land.

The fact that I was totally blind made no difference at all. At the age of ten, shortly after moving to the United States, I became seriously interested in shells. Almost immediately I started my own collection, which soon grew to include all manner of other objects of natural history. My parents and brother were enthusiastic; they read aloud, transcribed, or dictated every book on natural history they could find.

The reactions of my teachers in the local public elementary school ranged from polite acceptance to genuine enthusiasm when I told them of my intentions to become a conchologist, a malacologist, or a biologist. If they thought about the incompatibility between blindness and biology, they kept it to themselves, or perhaps they expected my obsession to be a passing fancy soon to be replaced by more realistic plans.

The interest in biology did not flag. As counselors more openly expressed their fears that I would be unable to find employment if I persisted in my plans to study biology, I entered Princeton University to concentrate on biology and geology. There I received strong support from nearly all my professors; they were giants in their fields, and their enthusiasm sustained my youthful confidence.

I applied to do doctoral work at Yale. When I arrived for my interview in the biology department, the director of graduate studies was more than a little apprehensive. During my talk with him, he took me down to the university's shell collection in the basement of the Peabody Museum. Casually he picked up two shells and asked me if I knew them. He fully expected me to draw a blank, in which case he planned to tell me as gently as possible that biology was not for me after all.

Fortunately, however, the shells were familiar to me. All of the misgivings of the director instantly evaporated. Thanks to his enthusiastic endorsement, I was able to enter

Yale with a full graduate fellowship that left me free to travel and to carry out an ambitious research project culminating in the Ph.D. dissertation.

After Yale, I joined the Department of Zoology at the University of Maryland at College Park in 1971, first as an instructor. Moving up through the academic ranks, I was appointed professor in 1980. Along the way, I married Edith Zipser, a fellow biologist whom I had met at Yale, and we had a daughter Hermine, who is now six. Very recently I accepted a new appointment to become Professor of Geology at the University of California, Davis.

What do I actually do in my job that seemed so improbable to the skeptics? Again the answer is simple. I do what my sighted colleagues do: research, teaching, and service.

My research centers on how animals and plants have evolved to cope with their biological enemies—predators, competitors, and parasites—over the course of the last six hundred million years of earth history. When I was still a graduate student, working at the University of Guam Marine Laboratory, I noticed that many of the shells I was finding on the island's reef-flats were broken despite their considerable thickness and strength.

It soon became clear that shell-breaking predators, especially crabs and fishes, were responsible for this damage. I began to suspect that many of the elegant features of tropical shells—their knobby and spiny surfaces, their tight coiling, and the narrow shell opening often partially occluded by knob-like thickenings—were interpretable as adaptations which enabled the snails that built the shells to withstand the onslaughts of their predators.

Most interestingly, the shells I had collected in the West Indies and the Atlantic coasts of South America and Africa seemed to be less well endowed with this kind of armor than were the shells from comparable sites in the tropical Western Pacific. Armed with these observations and hypotheses, I applied for funding from the National Science Foundation to continue my work upon my arrival at Maryland.

When the program director called me to say that I would be funded, he also informed me that the Foundation would not sponsor my proposed field work in the Indian Ocean because he could not conceive of a blind person's doing field work. I reminded him that I had already worked in field situations throughout the tropics, and that the proposed research critically depended on the work in the Indian Ocean. After a few minutes of conversation he relented and awarded me the full amount.

How do I do my research? It is a combination of field, laboratory, museum, and library work that has taken me all over the world to coral reefs, mangrove swamps, mud-flats, rock-bound open coasts, deserts, rain forests, research vessels, marine biological stations, secret military installations, great libraries, and big-city museums.

I make large collections of specimens in the field, work with living animals in laboratory aquaria, measure shells in museums and in my own very large research collection, and read voraciously. Wherever I go I am in the company of a sighted assistant or colleague.

Often this is my wife, but there are many others as well. There is nothing unusual about this; every scientist I know has assistants. I keep detailed field and laboratory notebooks in Braille, usually written with slate and stylus.

Once a week I go to the U.S. National Museum of Natural History, part of the Smithsonian Institution in Washington in order to work with the outstanding collection of mollusks and to peruse carefully all the scientific periodicals that came into the library the previous week. While my reader reads to me, I transcribe extensive notes on the Perkins Brailler. Sometimes I will make just a few notations of the main point of a scientific paper, but at other times I transcribe all the data contained in a paper. My Braille scientific library now comprises more than eight thousand publications compiled in more than one hundred forty thick Braille volumes.

Like many of my colleagues, I spend a great deal of time writing. First, I prepare drafts on the Perkins Brailler, using the seemingly inexhaustible supply of memos and announcements that flood my mailbox daily. Once I am satisfied with the text, I type the manuscript on an ink typewriter. An assistant proofreads and corrects the manuscript, which is then submitted to an appropriate scientific periodical or book publisher for a thorough evaluation.

In all my work I find Braille to be vastly more efficient than any other form of communication. I also prefer live readers to tape recorders. How can you ask a machine to spell words, to ferret out a detail in a graph or table, and most importantly to skip whole sections or to scan the text for a particular point?

Teaching has always been inextricably intertwined with research for me. I can point to several papers that would not have been written were it not for the fact that I was forced to think about problems in connection with a lecture on a topic quite far removed from my immediate research interests.

Over the years I have taught a great variety of courses—animal diversity, evolutionary biology, ecology, marine ecology, malacology, the mathematics and physics of organic form, and a seminar on extinction—ranging from the introductory to the advanced graduate level.

In the large introductory courses, teaching assistants take charge of the laboratory sections and help in grading papers. Again, there is nothing unusual in this. Professors in science departments at most universities depend heavily on teaching assistants. Like other research-oriented professors, I train graduate students. Thus far, seven students have received their Ph.D. degrees under my direction.

The service part of the job is highly varied as well. There are the inevitable committee meetings and the many tasks that help make the department or the university run smoothly. I head search committees to find new faculty members, I conduct reviews of faculty performance, and I write as few memos as I can. An important service to the profession is the review of dozens of manuscripts and grant proposals. If one writes them, one ought to be willing to review them as well.

Of course, science isn't all fun and games. Science is competitive; it is hard work, full of tedious calculations, revising manuscripts for the nth time, of coping with the disappointment of having a cherished paper or grant proposal summarily rejected, and of quibbling about grades with a frustratingly inept student. Nobody in science is exempt from pressures and feelings such as these, but in the end the work is immensely rewarding and intellectually fulfilling.

In short, there is nothing about my job that makes it unsuitable for a blind person. Of course, there are inherent risks in the field work; I have been stung by rays, bitten by crabs, and detained by police who mistook my partner and me for operatives trying to overthrow the government of their African country, and I have slipped on rocks, scraped my hand on sharp oysters and pinnacles of coral, and suffered from stomach cramps.

There isn't a field scientist alive or dead who hasn't had similar experiences. Life without risk is life without challenge; one cannot hope to understand nature without experiencing it firsthand. The blind, no more than the sighted, must act sensibly and with appropriate caution. Along with independence comes the responsibility of assuming risks.

What would I say to a blind person who is contemplating a career in science? Very simple. I would tell that person exactly what I would tell a sighted one: Love your subject, be prepared to work hard, don't be discouraged by doubters and by the occasional failure, be willing to take risks, get as much basic science and mathematics as you can take, and perhaps above all display a reasoned self-confidence without carrying a chip on your shoulder.

You will need stamina, good grades, the support of influential scientists, and a willingness and ability to discover new facts and new ideas. It is not enough to do well in courses; one must make new observations, design and carry out tests of hypotheses that have been carefully thought out, and interpret and present the results in such a way that the work is both believable and interesting to others. Science is not for everyone, but I can think of no field that is more satisfying.

What would I say to the educational establishment? I would tell them that the prevailing attitudes about science and the blind must be reformed. For too long the scientifically inclined blind have been steered only toward the social sciences and other "safe" disciplines, and away from fields in which laboratory and outdoor studies are important.

I believe that the chief factor holding the blind back from science is ignorance, not only by virtue of woefully inadequate reading materials in the schools and libraries, but also because of the pervasive fear and discouragement by the establishment to let the blind observe nature firsthand. I once met a blind woman who professed an interest in biology, yet she had never been encouraged to touch the spiny leaves of the holly.

Observation is the first, and in many ways the most important, step in a scientific inquiry. Without the freedom and encouragement to observe, a blind person (or anyone else, for that matter) is subtly but decisively turned away from science.

The key to this freedom is equality, and the key to equality is opportunity and respect. The National Federation of the Blind has long championed the philosophy that the blind are fully as capable as the sighted given sufficient opportunity and training. Education with this philosophy as its cornerstone is built on the assumption that no discipline is closed to the blind. By a logical extension, this basic respect will open more doors to the world of science as we continue to work for full participation in society.

If you or a friend would like to remember the National Federation of the Blind in your will, you can do so by employing the following language:

"I give, devise, and bequeath unto National Federation of the Blind, 1800 Johnson Street, Suite 300, Baltimore, Maryland 21230, a District of Columbia nonprofit corporation, the sum of $ --- (or "--- percent of my net estate" or "The following stocks and bonds: ---") to be used for its worthy purposes on behalf of blind persons."

National Federation of the Blind
You can help us spread the word...

...about our Braille Readers Are Leaders contest for blind schoolchildren, a project which encourages blind children to achieve literacy through Braille.

...about our scholarships for deserving blind college students.

...about Job Opportunities for the Blind, a program that matches capable blind people with employers who need their skills.

...about where to turn for accurate information about blindness and the abilities of the blind.

Most importantly, you can help us by sharing what you've learned about blindness in these pages with your family and friends. If you know anyone who needs assistance with the problems of blindness, please write:

Marc Maurer, President
1800 Johnson Street, Suite 300
Baltimore, Maryland 21230-4998
Your contribution is tax-deductible.